DISCOVER
THE PLANETS

Written by Cynthia Pratt Nicolson
Illustrated by Bill Slavin

Kids Can Press

Many thanks to Dr. Jaymie Matthews at the University of British Columbia for generously sharing his scientific expertise and his enthusiasm for the wonders of space.

 ™ Kids Can Read is a trademark of Kids Can Press Ltd.

Text © 1998 Cynthia Pratt Nicolson
Illustrations © 1998 Bill Slavin
Revised edition © 2005

Kids Can Press acknowledges the financial support of the Government of Ontario, through the Ontario Media Development Corporation's Ontario Book Initiative; the Ontario Arts Council; the Canada Council for the Arts; and the Government of Canada, through the BPIDP, for our publishing activity.

Published in Canada by
Kids Can Press Ltd.
29 Birch Avenue
Toronto, ON M4V 1E2

Published in the U.S. by
Kids Can Press Ltd.
2250 Military Road
Tonawanda, NY 14150

www.kidscanpress.com

Adapted by David MacDonald and Cynthia Pratt Nicolson from the book *The Planets*.

Edited by Jennifer Stokes
Designed by Sherill Chapman
Educational consultant: Maureen Skinner Weiner, United Synagogue Day School, Willowdale, Ontario

Photo Credits
All photos used courtesy of NASA.

Printed and bound in China

The hardcover edition of this book is smyth sewn casebound.
The paperback edition of this book is limp sewn with a drawn-on cover.

CM 05 0 9 8 7 6 5 4 3 2 1
CM PA 05 0 9 8 7 6 5 4 3 2 1

Library and Archives Canada Cataloguing in Publication

Nicolson, Cynthia Pratt
    Discover the planets / written by Cynthia Pratt Nicolson ; illustrated by Bill Slavin.

(Kids Can read)
Adaptation of author's The planets.
ISBN 1-55337-825-3 (bound).   ISBN 1-55337-826-1 (pbk.)

1. Planets — Juvenile literature. I. Slavin, Bill II. Nicolson, Cynthia Pratt. Planets. III. Title. IV. Series: Kids Can read (Toronto, Ont.)

QB602.N525 2005   j523.4   C2004-906885-7

Kids Can Press is a ℓ☺ⲣЈЅ™ Entertainment company

CONTENTS

OUR SOLAR SYSTEM

What do you see when you look up at the night sky? Do you see lots of twinkling stars? Look carefully, and you might also find one or two dots of light that don't twinkle. These glowing dots are planets.

What is a planet?

A planet is like a huge ball that travels around a star. Earth is a planet. It travels around a star that we call the Sun.

There are eight other planets that travel around the Sun. These planets are Mercury, Venus, Mars, Jupiter, Saturn, Uranus, Neptune and Pluto.

The Sun is one of many stars in space. The Sun is like a burning ball of fire.

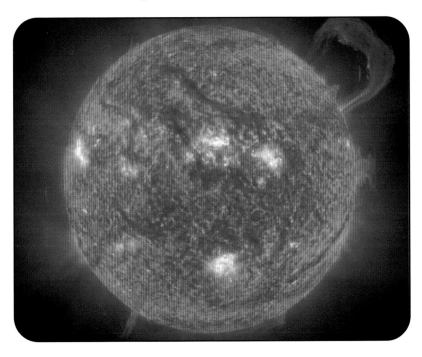

What is the solar system?

The solar system is made up of the Sun and the planets traveling around it. Below is a picture of our solar system.

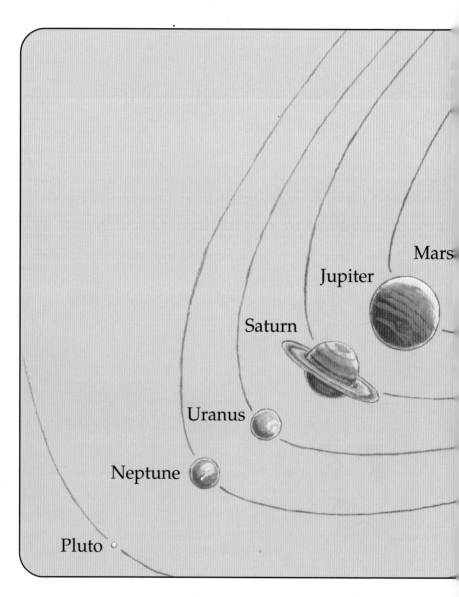

Mars

Jupiter

Saturn

Uranus

Neptune

Pluto

The nine planets of our solar system circle the Sun.

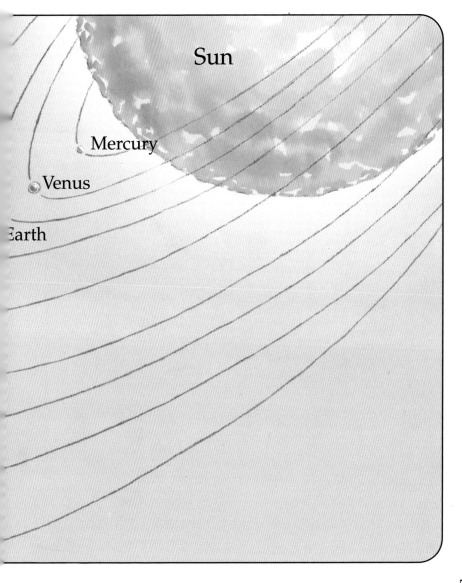

Why do planets look bright?

When fire burns, it makes light. That is why the flame on a candle helps you to see at night. Our burning Sun makes a lot of light.

Planets aren't burning, so they don't make any light. But the light from the Sun shines on the planets. This makes the planets glow.

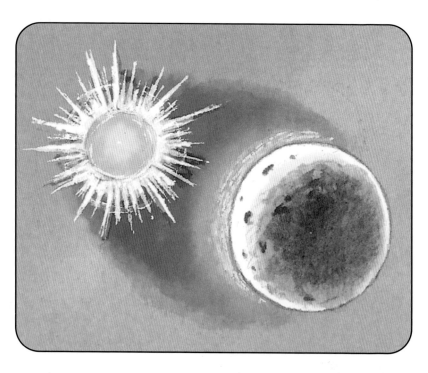

Part of this planet is bright because light from the Sun is shining on it.

How do planets move?

A planet moves in two ways at the same time.

It spins like a top.

As a planet spins, it also circles the Sun.
The path it takes is called the planet's orbit.
See the lines around the Sun in the picture
below? These lines show the orbits of the
different planets.

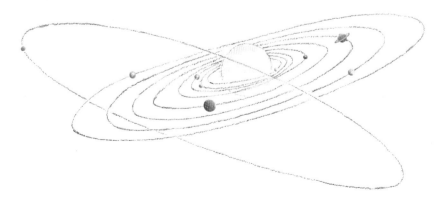

How big is our solar system?

Our solar system is huge! Imagine you were traveling on a jet plane from the Sun. It would take you 18 years to reach Earth.

Once you reached Earth, it would take you eight more years to get to Mars. Then you would have to fly for another 66 years to get to Jupiter. Getting all the way to Pluto would take 700 years!

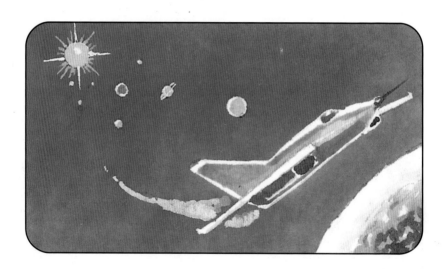

Are the planets all the same size?

Some planets are much bigger than Earth. Other planets are much smaller than Earth. This chart shows you the planets from biggest to smallest.

1	Jupiter (the biggest planet)	
2	Saturn	
3	Uranus	
4	Neptune	
5	Earth	
6	Venus	
7	Mars	
8	Mercury	
9	Pluto (the smallest planet)	

How can we compare the sizes of the planets?

We can use foods to compare the sizes of different planets. Let's imagine that Earth is the size of a cherry. This chart gives you an idea of how big the other planets are when we compare them to Earth.

The planet ...	would be as big as ...
Jupiter	a small watermelon
Saturn	a cantaloupe
Uranus	a large apple
Neptune	a large apple
Venus	a cherry
Mars	a small raspberry
Mercury	a pea
Pluto	a peppercorn

If the planets were the sizes of the foods shown here, the Sun would be as big as a large van.

MERCURY

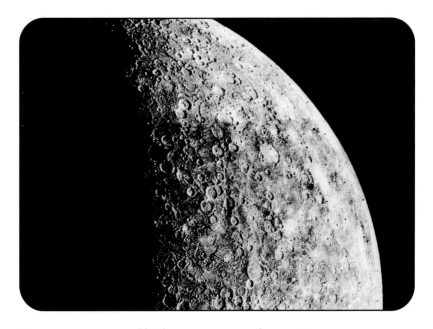

Do you see all those round spots on Mercury? Those spots are called craters. The craters were made when large pieces of rock that fly through space crashed into the planet.

The land on Mercury also has tall mountains, steep cliffs and large, flat areas.

Mercury Facts

- Mercury takes just 88 days to make its orbit around the Sun. That's fast!

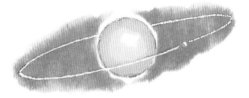

- Mercury is the closest planet to the Sun. The side of Mercury that faces the Sun is very hot. The other side is very cold.

- Mercury is only a little bigger than our moon.

VENUS

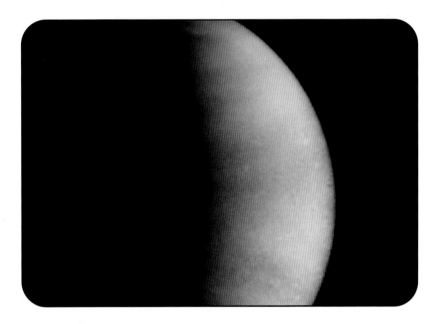

When you look at a photo of Venus, all you really see are the thick clouds that cover the planet.

Venus is so hot that if you went there your spacecraft would melt! A very hot day on Earth might be 40°C (104°F). A very hot day on Venus might be 460°C (860°F).

Venus Facts

- Venus takes just over 224 days to make its orbit around the Sun.

- The photo below shows circles on Venus. These circles were made by lava from volcanoes.

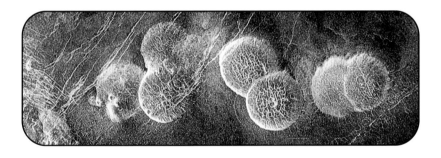

- Venus is sometimes called Earth's twin because it is almost the same size as Earth.

EARTH

Earth is the only planet in our solar system where people, plants and animals can live. Earth has the air and water we need.

Earth also has the right temperatures for living things. If Earth were closer to the Sun, it would be too hot. If Earth were farther away from the Sun, it would be too cold.

Earth Facts

- Earth makes its orbit around the Sun in about 365 days. That's one year.

- Earth has one moon. The Moon makes its orbit around Earth in 28 days. That's about one month.

- It takes about eight minutes for sunlight to travel from the Sun to Earth.

MARS

Mars is sometimes called "the red planet." That's because the surface of Mars is reddish brown, like rust. The white area at the top of the photo is ice.

People have never landed on Mars. But space probes have been sent there to help us learn more about this planet. A space probe is a spacecraft that has no astronauts on it.

Mars Facts

• Mars makes its orbit around the Sun in 687 days.

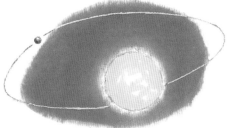

• Mars has two moons. These moons aren't round like Earth's moon. Instead, they are shaped like lumpy potatoes.

• Mars has a huge volcano called Olympus Mons. This volcano is three times taller than the tallest mountain on Earth.

JUPITER

Jupiter is the largest planet in our solar system. More than 60 moons make their orbit around Jupiter. Many of these moons are very small.

Jupiter Facts

• It takes Jupiter almost 12 years to make its orbit around the Sun.

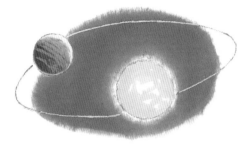

• Like all planets, Jupiter spins as it travels around the Sun. Jupiter spins more than twice as fast as Earth does.

• Jupiter is so big that all the other planets in our solar system could fit inside it.

SATURN

Many people think that the rings around Saturn make it the most beautiful planet in our solar system.

Saturn's rings are made up of dust and pieces of ice. Some of these pieces are as small as a pea. Other pieces are as large as a house.

Saturn Facts

• It takes Saturn almost 30 years to make its orbit around the Sun.

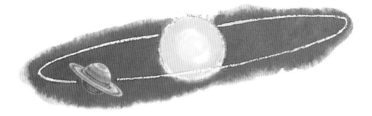

• Saturn is the second largest planet in our solar system. Jupiter is the largest planet.

• Saturn has more than 30 moons. You can see six of them below.

URANUS

Like Saturn, Uranus has rings around it. The rings around Uranus are darker and harder to see than Saturn's rings.

Uranus is a very windy planet. The winds on this planet are much stronger than the winds on Earth.

Uranus Facts

• Uranus takes 84 years to make its orbit around the Sun.

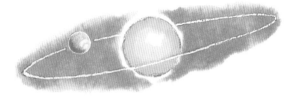

• Uranus is the only planet that spins on its side.

• Uranus has more than 20 moons. The photo below shows what the land on one of the moons looks like.

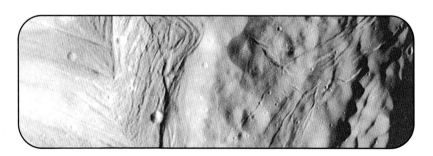

NEPTUNE

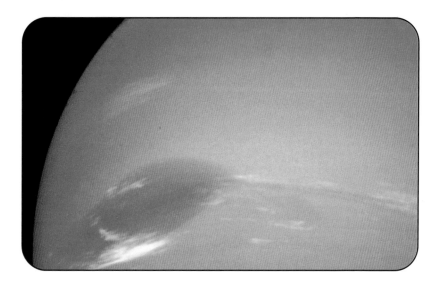

Neptune is blue, like the oceans on Earth. Do you see the white cloud at the bottom of this photo? This cloud moves quickly around the planet, so scientists call it "the scooter."

Neptune is freezing cold and very windy. It has the strongest winds of all the planets in our solar system.

Neptune Facts

• It takes Neptune almost 165 years to make its orbit around the Sun.

• In 1989, a space probe called Voyager 2 flew close to Neptune.

• Neptune has more than 10 moons. The photo below shows that the land on one of the moons looks like the outside of a cantaloupe.

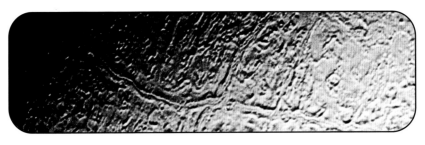

PLUTO

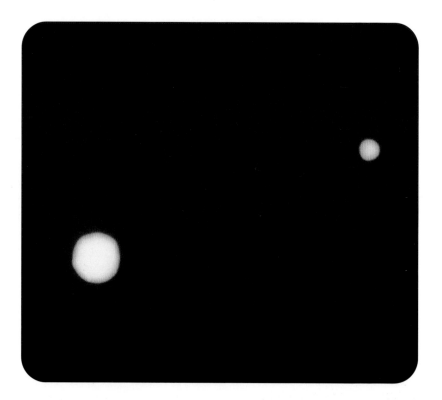

In this photo, Pluto is the large white dot. The smaller dot is Pluto's moon.

Pluto is the planet that is farthest away from the Sun. This makes it a very cold planet. The land on Pluto is rocky and icy.

Pluto Facts

• Pluto has a huge orbit. It takes Pluto over 247 years to travel around the Sun.

• Pluto is the smallest planet. It's smaller than Earth's moon. Pluto is like the baby planet in our solar system.

• When Pluto travels around the Sun, its orbit is tilted compared to the orbits of the other planets.

←Pluto

WHY DO WE STUDY THE PLANETS?

Every planet is different. Some are tiny and others are huge. Some are very hot and others are freezing cold. Only one planet is just right for people, plants and animals — and that planet is Earth.

Scientists have learned a lot about planets, but there is still much more to discover. Learning about other planets can help us take care of Earth, our own special planet!